DON'T GIVE UP THE SHIP

by Laura Neill

Uproar Theatrics

LICENSING & PRODUCTION INQUIRIES
Uproar Theatrics, LLC.
hello@uproartheatrics.com | www.UproarTheatrics.com

Characters

DIANA   40s-50s, acts as COMMODORE OLIVER HAZARD PERRY, 20s

OLIVE   20s, Diana's daughter, acts as Perry's Lieutenant SAUNDERS, 20s

MARTHA   20s, Diana's daughter, acts as Perry's nemesis ELLIOT, 30s

LIZZIE   20s, Diana's nurse and lover, acts as Perry's wife ELIZABETH C. MASON, 20s

JEFF   40s-50s, Diana's ex-husband, acts as Perry's son OLLIE HAZARD, 4

Setting

Diana's house in Rhode Island, which Diana imagines alternately as a nineteenth-century ballroom, Lake Erie, and a pirate ship

Props

All props should be things that could be found in a contemporary household. Optimally, the sword is a Swiffer with the end taken off.

A Note on Punctuation

… in the middle of a line indicates a beat or change in thought.
… at the end of a line indicates a trail-off.
— indicates an interruption or quick switch.
/ indicates overlap of lines.
" " indicates that a character is taking on language that belongs to another person. The words are either unfamiliar or over-exaggerated.

DON'T GIVE UP THE SHIP premiered with Fresh Ink Theatre in Boston, MA, February 2017. The performance was directed by Josh Glenn-Kayden, with sets by Madelynne Hays, costumes by Elizabeth Rocha, lights by Harrison Pearse Burke, sound by Andrew Duncan Will, props by Kelly Smith and Julia Fioravanti, dramaturgy by Jessica Foster, and choreography by Rachael MacAskill. The stage manager was Vivian Yee. The cast was as follows:

Diana... Alex Alexander
Lizzie...Hayley Spivey
Martha..Tonasia Jones
Olive... Louise Hamill
Jeff.. Robert Cope

To discover more plays by Laura Neill,
visit https://www.laura-neill.com.

Act One

Scene One

> *(At Rise: In darkness, the sounds of a storm. A sudden squall. Wind builds to a howl; waves rise to a crash. The music of the storm fades to hospital beeps. Lights up on DIANA's sprawled form on a hospital bed. Enter JEFF. He hesitates, then leaves a book next to DIANA's pillow.)*

> *(JEFF looks at DIANA for a moment and doesn't know what to do. He awkwardly picks the book up again and flips through its pages. People read to sick people, right?)*

JEFF

The Life of Commodore Oliver Hazard Perry, by Alexander Slidell Mackenzie.

Among the noblest of a nation's possessions is the memory of her great men. In the lowest state of degradation to which a nation may be reduced by her own degenerate profligacy, or by external causes which she cannot control, the memory of her mighty dead serves to solace her regrets, and to stimulate the noblest of the living to imitate their example.

> *(JEFF feels stupid. He sighs, shuts the book, and moves to exit.)*

> *(MARTHA enters.)*

MARTHA

How is she?

JEFF

Martha. Hi. Good.

MARTHA

You got her a book? That's sweet.

JEFF

I guess.

MARTHA

It's sweet.

JEFF

It was the only one in the gift shop that didn't… there were a lot of trashy romance novels.

MARTHA

…You're… reading to her?

JEFF

No, I was just--

MARTHA

It's a good idea.

JEFF
(a really bad joke)
If she hears my voice she might not / come back.

MARTHA

/ Daaad.

JEFF

I meant— I'm sure she'll wake up soon.

MARTHA

I'm sure she appreciates it.

                    JEFF

Right.

                   MARTHA

Do you want to join me?

                    JEFF

Coffee?

                   MARTHA

I'm going to pray.

                    JEFF

Oh. Thank you, but... according to your mother, I'm the
Antichrist, so…

                   MARTHA

Dad. Don't say that.

                    JEFF

I just meant— …Are you sure you don't—

                   MARTHA

I can't drink any more coffee.

                    JEFF

Maybe you should get some sleep.

                   MARTHA

I'm fine.

                    JEFF

You need sleep.

                   MARTHA

I'll be fine.

JEFF

Okay. …I'm gonna hit up the caffeine. Call me if anything changes.

(MARTHA and JEFF hug awkwardly. JEFF exits. MARTHA kneels.)

MARTHA

Hail Mary, full of grace, the Lord is with thee.

(MARTHA stops. She's not in it. She opens her eyes, shakes her hands out, and tries again.)

Hail Mary, full of grace.
The Lord is with thee.
Blessed art thou amongst women,
and blessed is the fruit of thy womb…

(MARTHA starts to cry. Or at least her voice shakes.)

… Jesus.

(MARTHA "pulls herself together" and stops her voice shaking, but she ends up barking the rest of the prayer out quickly.)

Holy Mary, Mother of God,
pray for us sinners,
now and at the hour of our—
now and always. Amen.

(MARTHA rests her head on the bed.)

Lord give me strength.
Holy Mother forgive me.

(MARTHA's eyes are closed. She rests. Enter OLIVE.)

OLIVE

Martha? Martha!

MARTHA

What?

OLIVE

Were you asleep?

MARTHA

No.

OLIVE

You fell asleep on the floor.

MARTHA

I was just... praying.

OLIVE

Oh. ...Is it working?

MARTHA

Don't mock me.

OLIVE

I wasn't. I just meant—...How's Mom ?

MARTHA

No change.

(Pause.)

OLIVE

Are you okay?

MARTHA

She's the one in the coma.

OLIVE

How long has it been since you slept?

(MARTHA ignores the question. She picks up the book JEFF left.)

MARTHA

Dad got her a nautical history book.

OLIVE

Martha--

MARTHA

Nautical history? Waves on the cover?

OLIVE

It's… relevant?

MARTHA

I swear, does he think before he—? Is he trying to rub it in?

OLIVE

I'm sure he didn't mean anything by it.

MARTHA

He never means anything by it.

OLIVE

It's a book. He's trying to be nice.

MARTHA

She almost drowned! Drowned, do you understand?

OLIVE

Yeah, I—

MARTHA

Drowned? In water?

OLIVE

She might be able to hear you.

MARTHA
(stage whisper)

Drowned.

OLIVE

I know. Will you *stop?*

(OLIVE sits MARTHA down.)

OLIVE

I know she almost—and I know you think—…No one
blames you.

MARTHA

What?

OLIVE

No one blames you at all.

MARTHA

Why would you blame me?

OLIVE

I don't! That's what I'm saying!

MARTHA

It was a squall. No one could have--

OLIVE

That's what I'm saying. ...I'm sure Dad doesn't blame you
either.

MARTHA

If no one blames me then why do you keep saying the word
blame? I didn't say blame. You started saying blame.

OLIVE

I didn't mean to. I felt like you were—with the "drowning,"
"in water," I mean—

MARTHA

I don't blame myself.

OLIVE

Then why are you acting like a crazy person?

MARTHA

I'm not acting like a crazy person!

OLIVE

You haven't slept!

MARTHA

Neither have you!

OLIVE

I was taking a nap when you called me!

MARTHA

And I was watching the Coast Guard give our mother CPR!
...I shouldn't have taken her out.

OLIVE

Martha...

MARTHA

What, did I think we were suddenly going to connect with each other via the magic of the summer waves? Mom doesn't even like sailing! She's never wanted to go sailing! But I rent a boat and take her out like we're stupid summer people or something—

OLIVE

She thought it was sweet.

MARTHA

It was supposed to be a gesture! I just wanted her to—

OLIVE

It was a nice gesture.

MARTHA

Don't patronize me! ...The clouds were getting messy, and she wanted to go in. She kept saying, I think a storm's coming up, and I thought she was just avoiding the conversation, and I didn't... She just kept talking about how Lizzie Masters got her nursing degree.

OLIVE

Lizzie Masters, the assistant coach from soccer?

MARTHA

Yeah. Lizzie Masters the assistant coach from soccer. Of all the random—

OLIVE

Why?

MARTHA

I don't know. Maybe she wishes she adopted her instead.

OLIVE

Martha!

MARTHA

Lizzie wouldn't've rented a stupid boat. Mom wouldn't be / in a coma.

OLIVE

/ It wasn't your fault.

MARTHA

…It was so cold. I didn't think the water would be so cold.

OLIVE

Was it as cold as this hospital? …I'm sorry. I mean—

MARTHA

Now isn't the time for stupid jokes.

OLIVE

I'm sorry. I'm just / scared.

MARTHA

/ Anyway, objectively, it was a poor decision, and I regret it. But I don't blame myself. Freak of nature.

OLIVE

Right. And you're not / scared?

MARTHA

/ We just need to be practical.

OLIVE

Practical?

MARTHA

We need to realize that she isn't necessarily going to—

OLIVE

She's not going to die!

MARTHA

—be the same. I was going to say, she isn't necessarily going
to be the same.

(OLIVE looks at DIANA.)

MARTHA

I'm just worried that... I called Lizzie and asked her to come
over and help.

OLIVE

Help with what?

MARTHA

I guess it's a good thing Mom was avoiding the subject. I
wouldn't have /

OLIVE

/ Hang on—

MARTHA

/ known that Lizzie was available. / All this hometown stuff
—

OLIVE

/ Just back up—

MARTHA

I just—

OLIVE

What kind of shape do you think she's going to be in?

MARTHA

Whatever it is, don't worry. I can... take care of the
expenses.

OLIVE

Who cares about the *expenses*? You're saying that Mom's
going to be—

MARTHA

It's not like *you* have the money to / take care of it.

OLIVE

/ What, do you want me to kiss your feet, Jesus? Back up!
What kind of shape do you think she's going to be *in*?

DIANA
(sitting up, sternly)

Gentlemen.

MARTHA

Mom?

OLIVE

MOM?

DIANA

I beg your pardon, gentlemen—I seem to have a codpiece.

OLIVE

You're awake!

MARTHA

Mom! You're awake! You're not--

DIANA
Did I not mention the codpiece? I beg you to stop addressing me as a woman!

OLIVE
She seems kind of... Mom? God, you're awake!

DIANA
I do wake up every morning.

MARTHA
...It's so good to see you, Mom, I--

DIANA
STOP CALLING ME MOM! I, as you can see--

MARTHA
You are incredibly high / on morphine.

DIANA
/ I, gentlemen... am a MAN!

MARTHA
Nurse!

> *(DIANA stands on top of the bed, jerking at her attached IVs.)*

OLIVE
OH, you're wrecking the IVs! Stop it--

DIANA
I will not be treated in such a manner! I am a lieutenant of the United States Navy!

MARTHA
A *lieutenant*?

OLIVE

Come DOWN, Mom.

DIANA

I and my codpiece and my VERY BIG SHIP / and I are
nothing short of--

MARTHA

/ It's just the morphine, / right?

DIANA
(over-macho)
Lieutenant Oliver Hazard Perry of the United States Navy!

OLIVE

Mom, you're scaring me.

MARTHA

You're ripping out your IVs!

DIANA

GENTLEMEN! I demand your salutes.

OLIVE

Please, / Mom--

MARTHA

/ We should find the / call button--

DIANA

/ I demand / your salutes.

OLIVE

/ Did you hear me, Mom? You're scaring / me.

DIANA

/ There is no place for fear in the United States Navy. *Your salutes.*

(OLIVE salutes.)

DIANA

Thank you, Saunders. You are going places.

MARTHA

Mom. It's us. Don't you recognize me?

(DIANA rounds on MARTHA, pointing the book at her.)

DIANA

Elliot, I'm warning you. Don't make me throw the book at you.

MARTHA

…The book?

(MARTHA takes the book from DIANA and looks at the cover.)

Scene Two

(Lights change. Music swells up—a battle march, or a macho-sounding mazurka. The bed becomes DIANA's bed; the hospital becomes DIANA's house. DIANA watches regally as OLIVE and MARTHA redecorate her bedroom, decorating with a nautical theme. MARTHA tries to hang a picture.)

DIANA

No, not there, Elliot! *There*, you incompetent.

(OLIVE rehangs the frame.)

DIANA

Thank you, Saunders.

(OLIVE and MARTHA continue to decorate. DIANA commands. LIZZIE rings the doorbell. DIANA settles on her now-nautical bed and reads.)

DIANA

And bring me a sword!

(OLIVE and MARTHA exit to the kitchen.)

MARTHA

Oh, I know, kids, let's get your mother a naval biography! Let's read it to her when her mind is in a fragile state! That can't go bad!

OLIVE

You don't need to blame Dad.

MARTHA

If only she'd listened to his suggestions this much when they were *married*--

OLIVE

Would that really have helped?

(They arrive at the door and let LIZZIE in.)

MARTHA

Thank goodness you're here.

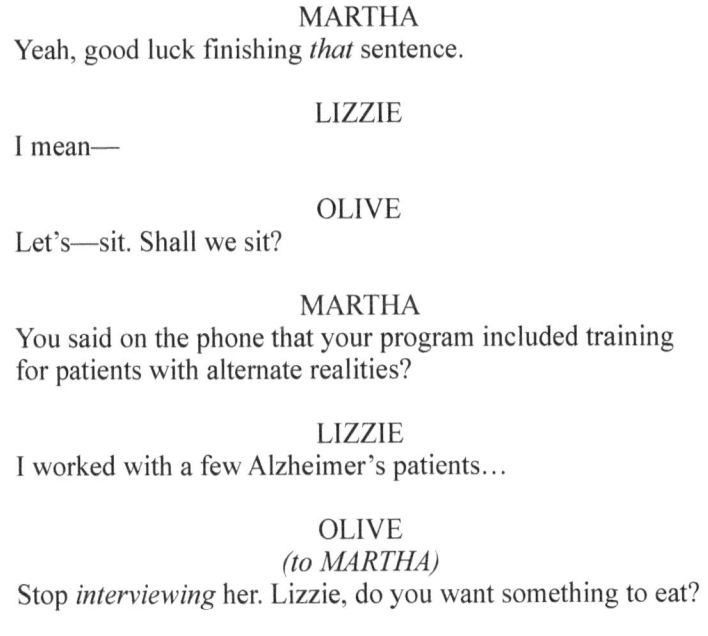

OLIVE

Hi, Lizzie.

LIZZIE

Hi.

OLIVE
(awkwardly)

It's good to see you!

LIZZIE

You too! I'm so sorry to hear that your mom is…

MARTHA

Yeah, good luck finishing *that* sentence.

LIZZIE

I mean—

OLIVE

Let's—sit. Shall we sit?

MARTHA

You said on the phone that your program included training
for patients with alternate realities?

LIZZIE

I worked with a few Alzheimer's patients…

OLIVE
(to MARTHA)

Stop *interviewing* her. Lizzie, do you want something to eat?

MARTHA

I'm not *interviewing*. I'm just trying to prepare her— *(to
LIZZIE)* She's handing out commissions left and right. It's all
in her precious "biography."

17

LIZZIE
So she's assigned you an identity?

MARTHA
Apparently I'm the most incompetent lieutenant in the history of lieutenants.

OLIVE
Do you want some cookies? I think we have some cookies—

MARTHA
She's started calling me Elliot. And Olive is Mr. Right-Hand Man over here. Darling Saunders. *(She looks at OLIVE offering cookies.)* Who eats stale Oreos, apparently.

LIZZIE
Well, that's something. I mean—for your mom. Patterns can be a good sign. ...They didn't cover this *particular* case in nursing school, but. The doctor said to humor her.

OLIVE
Well, her bedroom is thoroughly humored.

MARTHA
Decked out from sails to rails in "Ah yes, I'm an insane 1812 war veteran" and "Look at my codpiece."

LIZZIE
You're taking this with a good sense of humor.

MARTHA
Am I?

OLIVE
We're up and down. She's up and down.

MARTHA

It's her brain chemistry that's / up and down.

OLIVE

/ Anyway, Lizzie, we're glad you're here. Do you want some tea?

LIZZIE

Oh, that's--

MARTHA

You can drop your things in the guest bedroom.

LIZZIE

Thanks. ...And that is? Sorry, last time I was here was—

MARTHA

Yes. Down the hall, second door on the left.

LIZZIE

Thanks.

OLIVE

I'll make some tea.

(LIZZIE exits towards DIANA's room.)

MARTHA

Well. That was mildly awkward.

OLIVE

You could be, I don't know, less blunt.

MARTHA

And what kind of small talk can we make? How's your mom? Well, ours is out of her mind. How was nursing school? Comes in handy now that our mother is out of her mind. How's work? Oh wait, you don't have a job, that's why you can come nurse our mother who is *out of her mind*.

OLIVE

You could *try*. You don't have to treat her like—

MARTHA

I'm not paying her to make small talk. ...Well, that sounded awful. You know what I mean. This isn't a youth soccer game anymore.

OLIVE

...The Oreos aren't *that* stale.

> *(LIZZIE mistakenly enters DIANA's room instead of the guest bedroom. DIANA sees her. In DIANA's imagination: Their eyes lock, and music plays, a romantic overture, a symphony. DIANA rises.)*

DIANA

Miss...

LIZZIE

Lieutenant.

> *(As the music plays, DIANA sweeps LIZZIE into a dramatic waltz, dancing her around the "ballroom.")*

DIANA

You shall be the light of my life.

(LIZZIE is swept back to her original position by the door. Re-set. The scene re-plays in real life: DIANA sees her. There is no music. DIANA rises.)

DIANA

Miss...

LIZZIE

Oh. Hi! Sorry. I'll be right back.

(LIZZIE shuts the door and exits down the hall to put her suitcase in her room.)

OLIVE

It'll be good to have Lizzie around.

MARTHA

Yeah, *she* can go to Target next time.

DIANA
(calling from her room)

Saunders! Elliot!

MARTHA

I'll finish the tea.

OLIVE

Thanks.

(OLIVE goes to DIANA's room.)

DIANA

Saunders, I demand an introduction!

OLIVE

I'm sorry?

DIANA

The most beautiful lady in the world just swept into my life, and no one will tell me her name.

OLIVE

Oh. You met Lizzie? Re-met her? Did you remember—

DIANA

Stop speaking like a peasant, you silly man!

OLIVE

I'm guessing you don't remember her.

DIANA

Where is she? Has she left the ball?

OLIVE

We're at a ball.

DIANA

Of course we're at a ball, Saunders. Where else do eligible young lieutenants meet the women of their dreams?

OLIVE

"Of course we're at a ball."

> *(Lights change. The world becomes a well-lit, chandelier-ed, music-filled ballroom. DIANA is in uniform; LIZZIE becomes ELIZABETH CHAMPLIN MASON, in a gown; OLIVE becomes SAUNDERS. DIANA/PERRY and SAUNDERS snap into position and survey the ball casually, pretending that they haven't yet noticed the beautiful ELIZABETH.)*

DIANA

My, but what a fine night it is, Saunders.

SAUNDERS

I'll agree with you there, Perry.

DIANA

This music! This dancing!

SAUNDERS

Sure beats the Admiral's sermons on how best to keep one's head above water.

DIANA

Oh, Lordy, don't remind me.

SAUNDERS

Looks like there are even ladies here.

DIANA

Well, of course there are. It wouldn't be a ball without ladies, Saunders, where are your manners?

SAUNDERS

Does one have to have manners when on shore leave?

(ELIZABETH has had enough of the "I don't see you" game and introduces herself to the gentlemen.)

ELIZABETH

Good evening, gentlemen. Mr. Saunders, I do not believe I have made the acquaintance of this officer by your side.

DIANA
(makes an elaborate bow)

Perry.

SAUNDERS
May I present Lieutenant Oliver Hazard Perry?

DIANA
I am most delighted to make your acquaintance, Miss...

SAUNDERS
Elizabeth Champlin Mason.

ELIZABETH
(makes an elaborate curtsy)
Please, call me Elizabeth, Lieutenant.

DIANA
(another elaborate bow)
A pleasure.

ELIZABETH
(another elaborate curtsy)
The pleasure is all mine.

DIANA
Saunders, I think we're in need of some wine.

SAUNDERS
Wine.

ELIZABETH
Yes, Saunders, do fetch us some, will you?

DIANA
Be a sport, Saunders.

SAUNDERS
Be a gentleman, Perry.

(Lights change. SAUNDERS becomes OLIVE again; ELIZABETH CHAMPLIN MASON becomes LIZZIE as her ball gown fades away. OLIVE, out of uniform, introduces LIZZIE.)

OLIVE

Mom? This is Lizzie. You remember Lizzie? She'll be taking care of you.

DIANA

Truly, most delighted to make your acquaintance, Miss Elizabeth Champlin Mason.

LIZZIE

Nice to meet you too, Diana.

DIANA

Lieutenant Oliver Hazard Perry, commissioned 1807.

LIZZIE

So sorry. Of course. *Lieutenant.*

DIANA

Saunders, that wine?

OLIVE

What wine?

DIANA
(wink, wink)
The wine you were getting for us...

OLIVE

Well. You're not allowed to have wine, but I have a strong chamomile that'll knock your socks off.

(No one laughs. DIANA again gestures for OLIVE to go.)

OLIVE

I suppose I'll leave you two to get acquainted. Lizzie, Mom. Perry, Elizabeth Champlin Mason.

LIZZIE
(aside to OLIVE)

His…

OLIVE
(aside to LIZZIE)

Future wife.

LIZZIE

His *wife*?

OLIVE

I'm sorry.

DIANA

Do stop whispering, Saunders! How rude.

OLIVE

Of course… "Perry."

(OLIVE motions at LIZZIE to ask "Is this okay?")

DIANA

You are enjoying your evening, Miss Elizabeth?

LIZZIE

Er... *(to OLIVE and DIANA both)* Yes, thank you. It's perfectly fine. Lizzie's fine.

(OLIVE exits.)

DIANA

Not quite formal, I see.

LIZZIE

I prefer my gentlemen at ease.

DIANA

Do you.

LIZZIE

Have you been at sea long, Lieutenant? Sanders was just telling me--

DIANA

Saunders?

LIZZIE

Yes, was just telling me you've been "away" for about forty-eight hours now.

DIANA

Oh, much longer, much longer than that. I was at Jacmel! I was stationed off Algiers!

LIZZIE

Well. That's a lot of travel.

DIANA

There's a lot of dedication behind this heart.

LIZZIE

Of course. Hooo-ah!

DIANA

I beg your pardon. I do not understand your meaning.

                    LIZZIE
Just a… light turn of phrase.

                    DIANA
As you wish, Miss Elizabeth.

                    LIZZIE
Really, Lizzie is--

                    DIANA
Might you care to dance?

                    LIZZIE
Dance?

                    DIANA
Take a turn about the hall.

                    LIZZIE
I'm not sure I dance.

                    DIANA
But of course you do! All the fashionable ladies of the
year 1807 take a turn about the hall with dashing
lieutenants of the United States Navy recently returned
from battle.

                    LIZZIE
You're remarkably self-aware.

                    DIANA
Pardon?

                    LIZZIE
Yes, "I'll take a turn with you, sir."

DIANA

Excellent.

(DIANA makes a low bow and flourishes her hand out for LIZZIE to take. LIZZIE takes the hand and begins to waltz with DIANA, awkwardly.

DIANA steps on LIZZIE's foot.)

LIZZIE

Oh!

DIANA

My deepest apologies, miss.

LIZZIE

No worries. I mean—"consider yourself forgiven, Lieutenant."

DIANA

Oliver, please.

LIZZIE

Oliver.

DIANA

You know, my dear... may I call you my dear? You look familiar...

LIZZIE

As do you... Oliver.

DIANA

Perhaps I have seen you in my dreams.

LIZZIE

Oh-kay.

DIANA

You look so beautiful with that bashful blush on your cheek.

(LIZZIE drops DIANA's hand and pulls away.)

I beg your pardon. I didn't mean to be ungentlemanly.

LIZZIE

Just hang on.

DIANA

I beg your pardon.

LIZZIE

I think, when I knew you before, you were... different.

DIANA

Different?

LIZZIE

My dreams didn't go quite this way.

DIANA

Dreams never quite do. ...Another dance, Miss Elizabeth?

LIZZIE
(a rejection, of sorts)
No, thank you. I'm quite all right.

(LIZZIE hurries out of the room toward the kitchen.)

Scene Three

> *(LIZZIE enters the kitchen to find OLIVE and MARTHA. She covers her embarrassment with confidence.)*

LIZZIE

"She loves me."

MARTHA

How absurd.

OLIVE

I'm so sorry. I didn't realize—

LIZZIE

I figured I'd get cast.

OLIVE

Okay. Is this going to be okay? I mean, are you freaked out?

LIZZIE

It's fine.

MARTHA

You're not freaked out?

OLIVE

I know you're not trained for this sort of thing, I mean--

LIZZIE

No one really is, are they? For love?

> *(MARTHA chokes on her tea.)*

I'm kidding, Martha. It was a joke.

MARTHA

I don't know how you can be flippant about this.

OLIVE

So you think you can do it?

LIZZIE

I'm trained for unexpected situations. I'm trained to watch
someone's intestines falling out onto the floor and know
which surgery they need. I'm absolutely fine.

MARTHA

This is a bit different from intestines.

OLIVE

I'm really sorry.

LIZZIE

It's fine! He's quite charming.

MARTHA

She. Let's not get too into it.

OLIVE

Would you call Mom charming?

MARTHA

I'm just saying—

LIZZIE

It's definitely strange.

MARTHA

Yes. *Strange.*

LIZZIE

But she's harmless.

OLIVE

Good. Good. I'm sorry. This is all so crazy!

MARTHA

It's a medical condition.

LIZZIE

Olive. Stop apologizing. This is my job.

OLIVE

Well-- "you have Lieutenant Saunders' gratitude."

LIZZIE

I guess the lingo rubs off on you.

OLIVE

That it does, Miss Champlin / Mason.

MARTHA

/ Thank you, Lizzie.

(MARTHA's phone rings.)

MARTHA

Excuse me. ...Hello? Yes, this is she.

(MARTHA exits.)

OLIVE

I'm sorry about... Martha, too.

LIZZIE

Martha?

OLIVE

I mean, she's--

LIZZIE

--the same.

OLIVE

Yeah.

LIZZIE

She was always the same. Coaching the whole team from the bench.

OLIVE

Just, now she has a fancy "wealth management" job to top it all off.

LIZZIE

Wealth management?

OLIVE

As far as I can tell, she takes money from the poor and gives it to the rich. You know, "Sheriff Martha Nottingham."

LIZZIE

Oh.

OLIVE

Mom's proud of her. Was... proud of her.

LIZZIE

I'm sure she still is.

(Pause.)

You know, I feel like I should mention—have you looked into any of the counseling services at the hospital? Because there are--

OLIVE

I don't think counseling would help Lieutenant Perry.

LIZZIE

For Lieutenant Saunders, I mean. It's a strange situation, you're handling it well but—

OLIVE

I'm fine. Lizzie! I'm fine.

LIZZIE

It would be perfectly normal not to be fine. I mean--

OLIVE

Don't worry about me.

LIZZIE

You're the same, too.

OLIVE

Am I?

LIZZIE

Giving up your popsicle so the new girl can have one?

OLIVE

God, you remember that?

(LIZZIE shrugs.)

You make me sound like I'm trying to be a martyr. —I really just didn't like the yellow ones. I'm really fine.

LIZZIE

I'm just saying, you don't have to be--

OLIVE

But I am.

LIZZIE

Good. ...Good.

Scene Four

> *(The bedroom. Music. DIANA sails around the room, bracing herself against bay swells.)*

DIANA

To starboard! To starboard! This one's not going to the yard, you bloody idiot! Have you ever heard of a joyride? We're taking this one to sea! Just for a moment. Just to feel the wind on our cheeks. Just to ride the swells, maybe fire a few warning shots, ready ourselves for battle. ...The British are coming, after all. The British are coming! And I, Lieutenant Oliver Hazard Perry, have received my commission to take part in the battle. ...It's time. A RIDE OF JOY! To the wide and open sea!

> *(JEFF, as little OLLIE, enters, carrying a small toy ship.)*

JEFF

To where, Papa?

DIANA

Oh. My darling.

JEFF

Where are you going?

DIANA

To the sea, my little one. At last.

JEFF

(running in circles so his ship can ride the wind)

Hurrah! To the sea!

DIANA

Oh, my darling. You cannot come with me.

JEFF

Why not?

DIANA

You have not received your commission.

JEFF

But I want to go.

DIANA

You are not quite ready.

JEFF

Papa! I want to go!

DIANA

It will be dangerous, my darling.

JEFF

Then why are you going?

DIANA

I must protect you. I must protect all of us.

JEFF

Well, protect me *here*!

DIANA

I cannot. Ollie—

JEFF

Papaaaaaaa!

DIANA

Calm yourself, please.

JEFF

Papaaaaaaaaa!

DIANA

Please--

JEFF

You're my Papa! You're my Papa!

DIANA

I am also an officer of the / United States Navy—

JEFF

You're my Papa! You're my Papa!

DIANA

I have to go!

JEFF

You're MY PAPA!

DIANA

Ollie, I have to GO!

(Present day. JEFF becomes his adult self.)

JEFF

Diana, calm down. I don't know what you're saying.

DIANA

You cannot come with me!

JEFF

I didn't mean to upset you—I just wanted to *talk* / to you--

DIANA

I have to lead the charge!

JEFF

What charge?

DIANA
(calling for Lizzie)

My LOVE!

JEFF

Diana?

DIANA

My love! I need you!

JEFF

Is it you?

DIANA

I need you now!

JEFF

I--

DIANA

For the last time, I NEED YOU!

JEFF

I need you too.

(LIZZIE enters.)

LIZZIE

Is everything all right? I heard yelling—

JEFF

I think I'm—getting through to her.

LIZZIE

Getting—/ through?

> *(DIANA sweeps past JEFF to kiss LIZZIE on the cheek.)*

DIANA

/ My love. At last.

JEFF

Oh.

DIANA
(to LIZZIE)

You must help me convince little Ollie that he can't fight the British just yet.

JEFF

Diana—

DIANA

He thinks he's so big and strong, you see, but he's so little.

JEFF

Are you serious?

LIZZIE

Lieutenant, who is this?

DIANA

Oh, love. It's our sweet darling Ollie.

JEFF

Diana, I'm trying to *talk* / to you.

DIANA

You're not ready, Ollie.

LIZZIE

Stop it, Lieutenant.

JEFF

Why do you keep calling me Ollie?

DIANA
(to LIZZIE)

Our son has forgotten his name.

LIZZIE

It's our son. Perry's son. I didn't know we had... / gotten there.

JEFF
(to DIANA)

/ I thought you were coming back.

DIANA

How old are you now, Ollie Oll? Coming on four?

JEFF

You've got to be kidding me.

LIZZIE

There's no rhyme or reason to it, she just—

JEFF

That's what this is? That's all this is?

41

LIZZIE

It's not *her*.

JEFF

I know. You're delusional. Right?

DIANA
(to LIZZIE)

Help me, my love. Tell Ollie he's not ready to come with me.

LIZZIE

He's a big boy, Lieutenant.

JEFF

Boy? Whose side are you on?

LIZZIE

It might help if you go along and hint--

JEFF

I can't go along, I'm not even teething yet! Diana! Look at me!

DIANA

NO, Ollie, you cannot come. He's becoming rather grumpy, my love. Can you see to him?

LIZZIE

I—

DIANA

Does Ollie need changing?

JEFF

Maybe I was expecting too much from you.

DIANA

(cutesy) Such a grumpy little boy.

JEFF

I mean, you're delusional.

DIANA

(slightly less cutesy) Such a grumpy little boy at heart.

JEFF

No, that's you. --That's YOU!

LIZZIE

Oh.

JEFF

This is a new low, Di.

DIANA

Come to Papa. Say goodbye, now. / It's time for the battle.

JEFF

/ I come to see you when you're sick, and you—

DIANA

Commmme to Papaaaa.

JEFF

Yeah, I'll say goodbye all right.

(JEFF begins to exit.)

LIZZIE

Wait.

JEFF

Why should I?

LIZZIE

She's ill. She doesn't know what she's doing.

JEFF

She knows exactly what she's doing.

LIZZIE

Lieutenant, I think Ollie is a little overwrought.

DIANA

Some sacrifices have to be made in a time of war, / my love.

JEFF

/ Like you ever sacrificed *anything*! I left my beautiful
thirty-year-old girlfriend to come and see you—

DIANA

I have sacrificed more than you know, little Ollie, dear.

JEFF

You're killing your daughters, you know that? You're
making them miserable. They thought you *loved them.* But
you can't love anyone, can you? You can't love anyone,
because you can't handle not being in control. Because
you're a *control freak*, Diana. You always have to be at the
helm of your own little "ship." *You* steer, *you* lead, *you* talk,
you decide what happens to our family. Well, I'm sick of you
being in control, you hear me? I'm sick of you. …I'm going
back to my wonderful new life.

(JEFF exits.)

DIANA

He's always so *angry* when he has to go to his room.

                    LIZZIE

Oh, Diana.

                    DIANA

My dear Lizzie, you're upset.

                    LIZZIE

You can't just…

                    DIANA

Ollie will be all right. He just has a little growing-up to do.
Or a lot.

                    LIZZIE

Diana?

                    DIANA

Lieutenant Perry at your service, my love. Why do you keep
calling me Diana?

                    LIZZIE

I don't know. Why did you keep calling him Ollie?

                    DIANA

He's our son, my love.

                    LIZZIE

Of course.

                    DIANA

And we're so proud of him.

                    LIZZIE

Right.

                    DIANA

If only he weren't such an idiot.

LIZZIE

Excuse me?

DIANA

Such a little four-year-old. They're so stupid, at that age. ...I'm going to pack for the battle.

LIZZIE

Lieutenant?

DIANA

There are places Ollie can't follow.

DIANA sweeps out, hurriedly.)

LIZZIE

So self-aware.

(OLIVE and MARTHA enter as the sound of JEFF's car leaving the driveway is heard.)

OLIVE

Where's Dad going?

LIZZIE

I think he meant to say goodbye to you, but--

MARTHA

What happened?

LIZZIE

He's our son.

MARTHA

I'm sorry?

LIZZIE

She pretended that he was four. Ollie Hazard. "Come to Papa" and everything.

OLIVE

Oh, God.

LIZZIE

It seems like they have some history.

MARTHA

You can say that again.

OLIVE

So he's, um—?

MARTHA

He's thrown a tantrum and gone back to *Clarice*?

LIZZIE

He mentioned something about going back to his girlfriend.

MARTHA

This all just feels familiar.

OLIVE

It's not the same. You know that.

MARTHA

I mean, we all know this is hard to deal with, but *we're* not finding someone else on OK Cupid and storming off the second she mentions a break.

OLIVE

That's not fair.

MARTHA

She casts me as her lieutenant slave "whom she hates with a burning passion," and *I'm* not flying off to California.

OLIVE

Just New York.

MARTHA

Lieutenant Elliot is a loyal coward. Lieutenant Elliot stands there and takes it. But Dad gets cast as her kid, who she loves, and *that's* just too hard to handle? Is he serious? He can't handle pet names and love?

OLIVE

You know, just because she's not calling you pet names doesn't mean she doesn't love you.

MARTHA

Are you listening? That's not what I'm talking about! I'm talking about *Dad*.

OLIVE

Right.

MARTHA

We need to be here for her! We all need to be here for her right now!

OLIVE

I mean, you'll be going back to work soon.

MARTHA

I'm not going anywhere!

OLIVE

Are you not?

MARTHA

Don't give me that! Don't pretend like this is my fault!

OLIVE

I didn't say it was your fault!

MARTHA

You're giving me the "are you not?" like you're accusing me of something—

OLIVE

I'm just saying maybe *you* should stop getting all mad about people leaving!

MARTHA

I thought we were on the same side!

OLIVE

There aren't any sides!

MARTHA

There are always sides!

> *(MARTHA's phone rings. MARTHA has to*
> *answer it.)*

Hello. Yes, this is she.

> *(MARTHA exits.)*

LIZZIE

…There's clearly a lot going on for both of you. I think… there's this counselor at the hospital, Steve, he's—he deals in family trauma. If I give you his number… will you talk to Martha about going?

OLIVE

Lizzie, I know you're trying to help, but... we don't have
family trauma.

Scene Five

> *(Lights up on DIANA's bedroom/ship. Storm
> sounds begin. Sections from Chopin's Raindrop
> Prelude play. The storm builds. Diana raises a
> flag that reads "DON'T GIVE UP THE SHIP"
> on her bed.)*

DIANA

The waves rise. The waves rise! The Battle of Lake Erie
must begin. We are sailing the Great Lakes—in the dark of
night—as a squall comes up. Lieutenant Elliot and the USS
Niagara over there. The newly commanding *Master
Commandant* Perry and the USS Lawrence over here. Both
ships rocked from the side--British cannonfire everywhere!
Deadly, deadly cannon that will spark our lifelong battle as
the coward Lieutenant Elliot does not bring his ship into
position. Are you ready, sailors? Let us
BEGIN!

> *(The stage has now thoroughly become a naval
> battlefield, the storm at full volume. DIANA
> reigns the stage atop the bed. OLIVE, as
> SAUNDERS, is aboard. MARTHA, as ELLIOT,
> takes his perch on a chair. He wrestles with the
> "tiller," the top of the chair, in an attempt to
> turn the ship. Cannonfire rings out, and will
> continue throughout this scene.)*

DIANA

Elliot! What do you imagine you are doing?

SAUNDERS

What should we do, sir?

DIANA

Get Elliot's attention!

SAUNDERS

Lieutenant Elliot!

DIANA

Shoot back, Saunders!

SAUNDERS

Yessir!

DIANA

ELLIOT! To starboard!

ELLIOT

The rudder's damaged! I can't turn her!

DIANA

What?

SAUNDERS

What shall we do, sir?

DIANA

Fire! Fire at Elliot if you have to! We're getting pummeled over here!

SAUNDERS

I cannot fire at / Elliot, sir!

DIANA

I KNOW THAT, SAUNDERS! ...Do I have to do everything myself?

(DIANA grabs the flag and climbs from the bed onto a chair.)

SAUNDERS
Sir! We cannot leave the Lawrence!

DIANA
We must! Elliot's got his head up his bum!

ELLIOT
What's your game, Perry?

SAUNDERS
But my cannon!

DIANA
There's no other way! To the Niagara!

(DIANA begins to "row" the chair over to the Niagara, with great effort. SAUNDERS holds on behind.)

ELLIOT
WHAT ARE YOU DOING, PERRY?

DIANA
BRING HER AROUND.

ELLIOT
I SAID, I CAN'T, PERRY--

DIANA
DON'T GIVE UP THE SHIP!

(CANNONFIRE. DIANA reaches the Niagara-chair and climbs up, pushing ELLIOT off as she does so.)

DIANA
To starboard we must GO!

(DIANA swings the "wheel" again and accidentally throws herself overboard. She lands on ELLIOT, who becomes MARTHA, and lights change. SAUNDERS becomes OLIVE.)

MARTHA
Mom! What are you doing?

DIANA
I've brought the guns around! Fire!

OLIVE
Mom! Stop yelling!

DIANA
Fire, Saunders!

MARTHA
You just jumped on me!

DIANA
Shut your mouth, coward!

OLIVE
Whoaohhh—kay. Guess we're—

DIANA
The rudder was NOT damaged!

MARTHA

Your rudder is damaged!

OLIVE

Oh, no.

(OLIVE goes and flips through the book, finding the Battle of Lake Erie.)

DIANA

Your cowardice is unpardonable, Elliot! You will face court-martial.

MARTHA

You jumped on me.

OLIVE
(trying to show MARTHA the book)
Okay—I found it, it's—

DIANA

I don't think you'll find Elliot's courage in there.

MARTHA

You just jumped on me, Mom!

OLIVE

Martha, it's okay. You just—it's the Battle of Lake Erie. You were on the Niagara.

DIANA

The British were approaching! I had to take control of the ship!

MARTHA

You always have to have / control of the ship!

DIANA

/ You know, Lieutenant Elliot, I am well within my rights to challenge you to a duel.

MARTHA

I'll challenge you to a duel. How about you make your own food? How about you pay for your own healthcare? Huh? How about you find yourself a mental institution instead of a half-baked—

OLIVE

Oh-kay. I think we need a liiiittle diffusion. Lizzie!

MARTHA

Don't call her. We don't need her for everything.

OLIVE

We need her for this.

MARTHA

I can handle my own mother's *abuse* all on my own. I don't need her fake girlfriend.

> *(LIZZIE comes to the door. MARTHA motions her away.)*

Please stay out!

DIANA

Do not speak to Mrs. Elizabeth Champlin Mason Perry in such a manner!

OLIVE

She knows who we're talking about?

MARTHA

Elizabeth Chamlog Matwich Perry? Yeah. She's definitely herself.

(LIZZIE starts to come in.)

Please stay out of this! For now. Just give me some space.

DIANA

Recant your words, Lieutenant! Recant your words and your cowardly behavior on the lake!

MARTHA

Oh, now we're on a lake! Great.

OLIVE

I told you, it's the Battle of Lake Erie, if you'd just—

DIANA

You forced me to give up the ship.

MARTHA

All my fault, right? You shoving me over was my fault? The War of 1812 was my fault? *The storm* was my fault?

DIANA

You and your ungentlemanly conduct forced me to give up the ship.

MARTHA

Mom, stop this. Look at me. I am your daughter. I am not a gentleman.

DIANA

No, Lieutenant Elliot. You are not. *(to OLIVE)* Kindly
inform the sometime lieutenant that he will face court-
martial for his actions on the lake and that he will face my
displeasure for his remarks about Mrs. Perry, which were
cowardly, inappropriate, and frankly none of his business.

MARTHA

Kindly inform my mother that she's an asshole.

(MARTHA exits. OLIVE hesitates.)

OLIVE

Mom—don't challenge her to a duel. Please.

DIANA
(with a sigh)
Oh, Saunders. Go after him.

OLIVE

Mom?

DIANA

That's an order, Lieutenant Saunders.

(OLIVE exits.)

Scene Six
(LIZZIE enters the bedroom.)

LIZZIE

Saunders is a loyal lieutenant.

DIANA

He thinks he understands me, but he doesn't.

LIZZIE

You did just attack her sister. His brother. His Elliot.

DIANA

Elliot offended your honor.

LIZZIE

Elliot is only trying to protect you.

DIANA

He has a funny way of showing it.

LIZZIE

She—he doesn't understand. ...Perhaps if you showed him more care. I believe he has great respect for you, and "perhaps he's hurt that that respect is not returned."

DIANA

You know nothing of this.

LIZZIE

I--

DIANA

As a matter of fact, Elliot will be proven wrong, and I will be promoted. Promoted, you understand? For my courageous conduct on Lake Erie I will be made a commodore!

LIZZIE

Oh. / Great.

DIANA

/ So as much as I love you, as much as you are my wife, I'll thank you to stop defending that man and stay out of it!

LIZZIE

Right. Sorry.

DIANA

I'm sorry. I'm sorry, my Lizzie.

LIZZIE

No, you're right. I'm just your nurse. It's none of my business. Clearly your daughters are none of my business.

DIANA

Everything of mine is your business.

LIZZIE

Would that be because we're married now?

DIANA

Well—yes.

LIZZIE

We skipped the ceremony, I think.

DIANA

I don't know what you're talking about, my love.

LIZZIE

I never said I do.

DIANA

You did.

LIZZIE

I didn't.

DIANA

But you did. I'm sure.

LIZZIE

But I didn't. I'm sure.

DIANA

Well. ... ...Will you?

(DIANA gets down on one knee.)

LIZZIE

Will I marry you?

DIANA

Yes. Please. ...It is Rhode Island. It's not that unusual.

LIZZIE

What?

DIANA

For a dashing young commodore to marry a beautiful young lady.

LIZZIE

Are you—? Your behavior was "most unbecoming."

DIANA

I've apologized.

LIZZIE

You need to apologize to Lieutenant Elliot, I think.

DIANA

He insulted you.

LIZZIE

He only asked me to stay out of a personal matter.

DIANA

No, Lizzie, trust me, he insulted you. If you only knew what
he is... if he only knew what you are...

LIZZIE

What am I?

DIANA

You are my everything.

LIZZIE

Well. Um. You won the battle!

DIANA

The battle?

LIZZIE

The battle of Lake Erie. You won. The British are
vanquished. You're a commodore. That's good, right?

DIANA

I suppose.

LIZZIE

Let us celebrate! You have won!

DIANA

I would much rather win your heart.

LIZZIE

Well.

DIANA

Will you say it?

LIZZIE

Say what?

DIANA

Will you marry me? Do you take this--commodore--to be your lawful wedded companion? In sickness and in health? Till death do us part? ...I didn't mean to skip that part, my love. I'm sorry. Do you take me? In sickness and in health? Please?

LIZZIE

I do.

DIANA

You do?

LIZZIE

I do.

(DIANA kisses LIZZIE. LIZZIE kisses, then remembers herself and pulls back.)

I will take care of you, Diana. That's what I'm here to do.

DIANA

Oh, my love.

LIZZIE

But I'm only here to... I'm not here to…

DIANA

I need you, my Lizzie. Please.

LIZZIE

I'm your nurse, Diana.

DIANA

You're my love.

                    LIZZIE

Is it you?

                    DIANA

It's me.

                    LIZZIE

This whole time--

                    DIANA

Your adoring and dedicated commodore.

                    LIZZIE

Of course.

                    DIANA

I love you.

                    LIZZIE

I need tea.

                    DIANA

Tea?

                    LIZZIE

I'm going to get some tea!

            *(LIZZIE backs away and out of the room, toward
            the kitchen.)*

Scene Seven

            *(In the kitchen, MARTHA is angrily trying to
            find the teapot.)*

                    OLIVE

I'm telling you, she didn't mean to / hurt you.

MARTHA

/ She meant to hurt me, *Saunders*. Weren't you paying attention?

OLIVE

She's insane, Martha. She's following the book!

MARTHA

Oh, no. She's still in there somewhere.

OLIVE

If you would just read the book—

MARTHA

I have this new invention called an iPhone, Olive.

OLIVE

But she's following the Alexander Slidell Mackenzie.

MARTHA

Our mother is physically attacking me and you think the *edition* matters?

OLIVE

Yes!

MARTHA

Lord our God preserve me.

OLIVE

There are some really interesting resources at the library, if you would just—

MARTHA

You work in Circulation, Olive! Don't get all high and mighty about the fount of knowledge with me!

OLIVE

Don't yell at me! I'm not the one who's attacking you!

MARTHA

Well, it feels like it!

OLIVE

Well… *(awkward)* That's too bad, because I'm not!

MARTHA

(hesitates, then gives up the fight to grumble)
…Just don't ever give her that sword.

OLIVE

Oh, come on. She wouldn't hurt you.

MARTHA

No, but she'd hurt Lieutenant Elliot. Where's the friggin tea pot?

OLIVE

Under the sink.

MARTHA

I *know* that!

(LIZZIE goes back to the bedroom without tea.)

DIANA

My love! You return.

LIZZIE

I decided against the tea.

DIANA

But why, my love?

LIZZIE

Um—

MARTHA
(so loudly she can be heard down the hall)
Where's the friggin tea?

DIANA

Come, my love.

OLIVE

In the top left.

MARTHA

I KNOW that!

LIZZIE

Right. Commodore--

DIANA
I've led men through ferocious battles and unending storms,
my love. I can lead us through anything.

(DIANA leads LIZZIE towards the kitchen.)

Peace and prosperity. Like the book says.

LIZZIE
The book? Do you mean the—

DIANA
The Good Book. The Bible. The guide to holy matrimony.

LIZZIE
I don't think we'll find a lot of peace.

DIANA

Ah, my love, don't be so glum. You are with me, and I with you!

(DIANA enters the kitchen, sees OLIVE.)

Saunders! Do give us your blessing!

OLIVE

My blessing?

DIANA

On our marriage, of course! We've renewed our vows.

MARTHA

Your WHAT?

OLIVE

Oh, boy.

DIANA

Our vows, you impudent man.

MARTHA

You had to take the sacrament.

OLIVE

…"Blessings be upon you."

MARTHA

You really had to--

DIANA

Thank you, Saunders. Very good.

MARTHA

The *sacrament*, Mom?

OLIVE

Weren't you the one just telling me not to get all high and mighty?

MARTHA

God is a little more important than *books*!

OLIVE

Right.

LIZZIE

…"What a delightful occasion it is." Let us celebrate with some tea.

DIANA

A brilliant idea, my love!

(MARTHA is clearly making tea already.)

MARTHA
(viciously)

I know! I'll make it.

OLIVE

Martha—

MARTHA

From knocking me over to *this*? Is she serious?

OLIVE

It's in the—

MARTHA

If you say it's in the book I swear I will hit you with this teapot.

DIANA

My darling one, what is Lieutenant Elliot doing in our kitchen?

LIZZIE

Let him be, my dear.

MARTHA

Stop calling her that!

LIZZIE

Let me do it, Martha?

MARTHA

I'm not paying you to call her pet names! I'm paying you to get her back!

OLIVE

Oh, Jesus.

MARTHA

Lord's name!

DIANA

Elliot, it's our wedding day. Please do be civil.

(MARTHA picks up the teapot.)

MARTHA

Civil? You want civil?

> *(She viciously pours tea "into" mugs, slopping water all over the counter. She places a mug in front of DIANA, slopping water all over the table, too.)*

I'll give you civil.

*(MARTHA exits the kitchen, headed toward
DIANA's room.)*

DIANA
Saunders, would you take this? I don't want anything that
man made.

OLIVE
Christ, Mom.

DIANA
"Lord's name."

OLIVE
Mom? Are you—

DIANA
Please do remember that I am your commanding officer,
Lieutenant Saunders.

> *(MARTHA enters DIANA's room and places a
> large cardboard box on the bed.
> She looks around for everything with a nautical
> theme and starts to put things in the box. She
> takes a picture of a boat off of the wall. Scenes
> run simultaneously in the bedroom and in the
> kitchen.)*

OLIVE
Sir, if I could mention… I know you're "rejoicing in your
nuptials," but I believe Lieutenant Elliot

OLIVE
suffers from the lack of your regard.

DIANA

As I suffer from his lack of regard for common decency.

LIZZIE

My dear.

OLIVE

Mom.

(MARTHA takes a knickknack of a sailor, takes an ocean-themed snowglobe.)

DIANA

Commodore.

OLIVE

Commodore. "Cannot you find it in the depths of your heart to reconcile with your loyal lieutenants?"

(MARTHA begins throwing the things in the box with more energy as she goes along. She eyes the sheets, which are patterned wavy blue.)

DIANA

I'm meant to be celebrating, Saunders. Victory on the lake! Victory in my heart! Leave Elliot alone.

LIZZIE

Saunders is concerned—

DIANA

Leave it ALONE, my love.

(OLIVE exits down the hall. LIZZIE begins to clean up the mess MARTHA made, in silence.)

Scene Eight

> *(OLIVE enters DIANA's room and sees that*
> *MARTHA is destroying the decor.)*

OLIVE

What are you doing?

MARTHA

Nothing.

OLIVE

"Nothing" is the best thing you could come up with?

MARTHA

All right, something. I'm finally doing something. I'm
moving some things around.

OLIVE

I can see that. Mom's pictures? Her sailor?

MARTHA

I'm cleaning up.

> *(MARTHA starts to strip the sheets again.)*

OLIVE

Wait! Stop!

MARTHA

Stop what?

OLIVE

You're... wrecking it!

MARTHA

I'm not wrecking anything. I'm looking out for Mom, here.

OLIVE

This isn't going to make her like you.

MARTHA

Either help me or get out.

OLIVE

She's going to be upset with you!

MARTHA

I think we already covered that ground!

OLIVE

More upset! She'll be more upset.

MARTHA

Good! Great. Then she'll be upset as herself. I bet
Commodore Whozawhatsit doesn't care about what kind of
sheets he sleeps on.

OLIVE

You realize she's not actually Commodore Whozawhatsit.

MARTHA
(*sarcastically*)

Yes. I'm faintly aware.

OLIVE

I mean—she'll get better—look, STOP THAT.

(*OLIVE keeps MARTHA from removing one of
the sheets.*)

MARTHA

IT'S FINE FOR YOU!

OLIVE

Come on, Martha--

MARTHA

Her precious identities work out fine for you! Finally the
favorite daughter! Finally the one she likes.

OLIVE

What do you mean, "finally"?

MARTHA

Isn't that what you've been after for years? Staying in town,
helping out, getting a local job like a good little child, trying
to get her attention.

OLIVE

Some people don't dream of world domination, Martha.

MARTHA

Some people just don't think they can achieve it.

OLIVE

I'm gonna remind you one more time that *you're not mad at
me*.

MARTHA

Right. Because no one's ever mad at perfect Olive.

OLIVE

Literally no one has ever called me that. ...You know,
Martha, Lizzie was talking about some counseling services /
at the hospital that might be good for you.

MARTHA

/ Lizzie? Lizzie! You're gonna listen to Lizzie? She's got it great, doesn't she? So sweet and lovely and the focus of all Mom's attention. Finally got the head coach to love her, huh? After years of mediocrity and settling for a cheap little trade degree, she's finally the best one in the room? She'll get the nice little nursing trophy?

OLIVE

Christ.

MARTHA
(a reminder)

Lord's name.

> *(MARTHA wrenches the sheet from OLIVE and continues taking things off the bed and dumping them into the box.)*

OLIVE

…She's insane, Martha! It doesn't mean / that she hates you.

MARTHA

/ Are you really going to tell me that it doesn't mean anything? That she yells at me, ignores me, pushes me over? How are you going to tell me that doesn't mean anything?

OLIVE

It's not / her fault.

MARTHA

/ She chose us! Her and dad! We're supposed to be a family!

OLIVE

We *are*.

MARTHA

Are we? Cause it feels like she's kicking me out.

(Pause.)

I don't know what I did, okay? I don't know. I don't know
what to do, I don't know how to help her, I don't know if she
even wants help. ...I don't think she wants help. ...If she
would just trust me.

OLIVE

Trust you?

MARTHA

Before the storm... during the storm...

OLIVE

What?

MARTHA

She wouldn't talk to me. Not when the winds came up. Not
with the sail. Not even when she went overboard, she—she
wouldn't take my hand. ...There was a moment where I think
she could've caught my hand, but she didn't. She just let go.

OLIVE

Do you think she meant to--

MARTHA

I don't know.

OLIVE

Jesus Christ. ...I mean… "Jesus Christ."

(A heavy pause. Then MARTHA shakes off her
thoughts and commences throwing things in the
box.)

OLIVE (cont)
But this isn't—I mean—would you please stop doing that?

(MARTHA is now searching under the bed for nautical items.)

MARTHA
(voice muffled, under bed)
Stop doing what?

OLIVE
Stop destroying—stop everything! Did you hear what you just said? You think she's... suicidal.

(OLIVE grabs the box and takes it away from MARTHA's reach.)

MARTHA
(voice muffled)
Give me my box back!

OLIVE
Stop avoiding the conversation!

MARTHA
(coming out from under the bed)
Give it to me!

OLIVE
No!

MARTHA
Come on, Saunders!

OLIVE
No, Elliot!

MARTHA

Don't call me that.

OLIVE

You started it.

MARTHA

No, I didn't!

OLIVE

Yes, you did!

MARTHA

I didn't say that she's suicidal. She's just in a different world.
And if destroying that world is what I have to do...

> *(MARTHA reaches over and takes the book from
> the nightstand. She tosses it into the box without
> breaking OLIVE's stare. OLIVE takes the
> snowglobe out of the box and puts it back on a
> shelf. MARTHA marches over, grabs the
> snowglobe, and tosses it back in the box.)*

OLIVE

Be careful with that.

MARTHA

Uh-huh.

OLIVE

It was Grandma's.

> *(OLIVE starts putting objects from the box back
> in their places as fast as she can. MARTHA
> counteracts this by putting objects back in the
> box as fast as she can. Sailor, snowglobe.
> Picture. Sheets. Picture. Book. Snowglobe.*

Picture. Book. Sailor. Sheets. Their actions
become more and more frantic until MARTHA
makes a sudden grab for the box.)

MARTHA

Give it to me!

(OLIVE doesn't let it go. MARTHA pulls hard.)

OLIVE

What are you--

MARTHA

Let go!

OLIVE

Martha!

MARTHA

I said let GO!

OLIVE

YOU let go!

(MARTHA lets go suddenly and OLIVE falls
back.)

Ow.

MARTHA

You okay?

(OLIVE takes out the book MARTHA threw and
tosses it back at MARTHA.)

Ow.

OLIVE

Serves you right. ... ...She doesn't love me either, you know.

MARTHA

What?

OLIVE

Saunders. He just gets ordered around, and occasionally they have bro talk. It's weird. It's awful. It's not Mom.

MARTHA

...Ollie...

OLIVE

I don't know why you think I'm in control. No one is in control here.

MARTHA

Except Mom.

OLIVE

I really don't think she is, either. *Please.*

MARTHA

So let's do something.

OLIVE

There's nothing we can do.

MARTHA

Help me bring her back.

OLIVE

The doctor said that we should / humor her.

MARTHA

/ The doctor said nothing. She's never seen this before. No one has ever / seen this before. Not with our mother.

OLIVE

/ I don't know if making up our own way is the / best idea.

MARTHA

/ This is our mother. If anything is up to us—

OLIVE

You think this will work?

MARTHA

If we don't do anything, we'll keep losing her. Do you want your mother back or not?

OLIVE

When you put it that way, it sounds—

MARTHA

She might be suicidal, Olive! Do you want her back or not?

OLIVE

OKAY!

(OLIVE grabs a book from the box and throws it across the room.)

MARTHA

Good arm.

(OLIVE and MARTHA partner together to destroy the room. MARTHA picks up DIANA's sailor and cracks it. OLIVE grabs a picture and slams it against the bedframe. MARTHA kicks the picture. OLIVE takes the wave sheets and tears them. MARTHA joins in. MARTHA scatters the wave sheets over the floor. MARTHA tears through DIANA's bedside table drawers and finds a lipstick. Somewhat viciously, she writes

*"HI, MOM!" on the headboard of the bed. Once
the room is completely destroyed, OLIVE places
Grandma's snowglobe back on the disordered
bed.)*

OLIVE
Something to remember us by.

MARTHA
Dear Lord. Please let our mother remember us.

*(The storm of music rises again. MARTHA and
OLIVE exit.)*

Scene Nine

*(LIZZIE enters the bedroom, sees the
destruction, and gasps. LIZZIE tries to fix
things, but has no success before DIANA enters.)*

DIANA
My love? …My God. Our home.

LIZZIE
Just a stray wind, my dear.

DIANA
A stray wind? A stray *wind*?

LIZZIE
Or, or, looters, after the battle.

DIANA
Our home is in Newport. The battle was in Ohio.

LIZZIE
Jealous privates from the army.

DIANA

A stray wind?

LIZZIE

We'll fix it. I'll get it all nice and tidy.

DIANA

How could they do this to me?

LIZZIE

Who?

DIANA

Why would they do this to me?

LIZZIE

Don't worry. I'm an excellent homemaker, just like all of the other navy wives from the 18th century. I'll get this cleaned up in no time.

DIANA

Nineteenth.

LIZZIE

What?

> *(DIANA walks to the bed and picks up the snowglobe.)*

DIANA

This was my mother's.

LIZZIE

Oh. That's—nice.

DIANA
They destroyed everything else.

LIZZIE
It's all right, my... my love.

DIANA
They wouldn't destroy this.

LIZZIE
Oliver? Did you hear? I called you my love.

> *(DIANA dashes the snowglobe to the ground. It shatters.)*

Oh my God.

DIANA
She wouldn't have approved of you.

LIZZIE
Oh my God. That was your mother's--

DIANA
Sarah Lawrence Perry never saw a snowglobe in her life.

LIZZIE
(*realizing*)
That was your... mother's.

DIANA
It's not important.

LIZZIE
I can fix it, I'll try to fix it—

DIANA

I don't need it. I need you.

LIZZIE

You can have both.

DIANA

I can't. ...They're jealous of you, my love! My... lieutenants. My cowardly, dastardly lieutenants. They don't know who you are, but they want their commodore back. They want someone to lead them without caring for himself. I cannot be that person anymore.

LIZZIE

...Why not?

DIANA

I don't know. Because they do things like this.

LIZZIE

"Lieutenants."

DIANA

Yes. Lieutenants. Even though they're grown, even though they're always pushing me away, even though they don't want to be here, always, they expect me to be perfect for them.

LIZZIE

Diana?

DIANA

When they come home, home must be perfect. I must be perfect.

LIZZIE

Diana.

DIANA

The honor of Commodore Oliver Hazard Perry must always
be intact.

LIZZIE

Oh. Yes.

DIANA

Tell me honestly, will you do this to me? Will you—

LIZZIE

I'm a healer... Oliver. I don't destroy.

DIANA

They destroy everything.

LIZZIE

They are... young...

DIANA

Please don't defend them.

LIZZIE

I am young too.

DIANA

I know.

> *(LIZZIE kisses DIANA, gently, at the side of her
> cheek, almost on her mouth.)*

You don't think you will... destroy my world?

LIZZIE

I think you've created mine.

(They kiss, on the lips.)

DIANA
I feel as though I have loved you for a long time.

LIZZIE
(to herself)
I probably shouldn't have done that.

DIANA
I love you the way the waves caress the bow.

LIZZIE
I shouldn't have actually—

DIANA
I love you the way the ocean loves the sky.

LIZZIE
Diana—

DIANA
I love you the way the Commodore loved his wife.

> *(DIANA and LIZZIE embrace passionately.*
> *Music rises; lights fade. In darkness, a*
> *symphony plays, then fades. From the silence,*
> *DIANA says:)*

When Oliver Hazard Perry and Elizabeth Champlin Mason
are both turned to dust--

LIZZIE
Yes—

DIANA
Will our souls still be intertwined?

LIZZIE

Yes, my love. ...Yes.

(All is dark and still.)

(End of Act One.)

Intermission

(When the lights rise for intermission, DIANA is gone, and LIZZIE is working to restore the room to being "shipshape." She puts the busted pictures back on the walls, tosses the torn wave sheets back on the bed—her efforts don't work, but she tries. LIZZIE then tries to smear the lipstick off of the headboard, but only succeeds in smearing the "H" so that the message reads "i, Mom!")

Act Two

Scene One
> *(As LIZZIE attempts to smear off the next letter,*
> *JEFF enters.)*

JEFF

Hi, Mrs. Perry.

LIZZIE

Oh! Hi.

JEFF

My daughters did quite a piece of work here.

LIZZIE

Yes... they did.

JEFF

I think they get that passion from her. I was always the
passive-aggressive type.

LIZZIE

Oh. … ...How was California?

JEFF

Nice, I hear. I didn't go.

LIZZIE

Oh.

JEFF

How could I? With her like this.

LIZZIE

Of course.

JEFF

Whatever she thinks of me, she knows I still love her.

(LIZZIE drops her paper towels, then scrambles to pick them up.)

She just gets under my skin. You know?

LIZZIE

Yeah.

JEFF

Must be strange, being her... wife.

LIZZIE

It's, I don't know--

JEFF

It was hard enough being her husband.

LIZZIE

...Yeah.

JEFF

Can't even imagine.

LIZZIE

So you two didn't leave it on... good terms? I mean, it's none of my business.

JEFF

We're fine.

LIZZIE

You're remarried?

JEFF

No.

LIZZIE

I'm sorry, I just heard Olive and Martha... I thought Clara--

JEFF

Clarice is not my wife.

LIZZIE

Oh.

JEFF

I gave her the book, you know.

LIZZIE

The Perry.

JEFF

Yeah.

LIZZIE

I guess she liked it. ...The history, you know—it must have resonated with her intellectually—

JEFF

How do you do it?

LIZZIE

Do what?

JEFF

Wife? To my wife?

LIZZIE

Ex-w—not that it's any of my—

JEFF

You just pretend to love her?

LIZZIE

I don't know, I—

JEFF

Does she pretend to love you?

LIZZIE

We just talk.

JEFF

Does she tell you you're pretty?

LIZZIE

We just... talk.

JEFF

Does she nag?

LIZZIE

No.

JEFF

You'll find out soon enough she likes to nag.

LIZZIE

I'm sorry, Mr.--

JEFF

Don't ever leave your socks on the floor.

LIZZIE

I'm the nurse, Jeff, I—

JEFF

Right! You're the woman in the relationship.

LIZZIE

Excuse me?

JEFF

You must tell her to pick up HER socks.

LIZZIE
(*snaps*)

Would you please stop?

JEFF

Well. Getting a little defensive?

LIZZIE

I just—why is everyone in this family trying to destroy her?

JEFF

What?

LIZZIE

You say you love her, and then you say things like that!

JEFF
(laughs angrily)
You seem very *opinionated* / for someone who--

LIZZIE

/ I'm sorry. It's not my place.

JEFF

You're right. It's not. ...You're young. When you've been
married for a long time... you'll understand.

LIZZIE
I don't think I'll ever want to tear her down.

JEFF
Good thing you're not really marrying her, then.

LIZZIE
But... I AM taking care of her. And this--

(Enter OLIVE.)

OLIVE
Dad. Martha's back. We need to talk.

JEFF
Coming.

LIZZIE
Should I—

JEFF
Why don't you take a rest, Lizzie?

OLIVE
Yeah. Lizzie, why don't you take a break?

LIZZIE
She asked me to fix it.

OLIVE
Well... Martha and I have decided not to.

LIZZIE
She can't sleep on torn sheets.

OLIVE
There are others in the hall closet.

LIZZIE

Fine.

OLIVE

Lizzie... leave the rest of it. Please.

LIZZIE

It's your call.

*(DIANA carouses through the hallway, singing
at the top of her lungs. She arrives loudly at her
bedroom.)*

DIANA

Whennnnnnn Brits are filling sea and sky,
When morale is low and seas are high,
The Uniiiiited States flag will fly!
DON'T GIVE UP THE SHIP!
Oh, don't give up the ship!
Oh, don't give up the ship!
When morale is low and seas are HIIIIIIIIGHHHHH,
DON'T GIVE UP THE SHIP!
(to LIZZIE)
My love! What a wonderful day!

LIZZIE

Truly, my dear?

DIANA

The Lieutenant Elliot and I went for a walk together... and I
pushed him in the lake!

OLIVE, JEFF, and LIZZIE

WHAT?

LIZZIE

You didn't—

DIANA

Oh, I'm just fooling you, my love. Just a little joke.

JEFF

Jesus Christ, Diana.

DIANA

Oh, look, it's little Ollie!

JEFF
(between his teeth)

Yes, that's me.

DIANA

Saunders, do take good care of him, will you? His mother and I need some alone time.

LIZZIE

Commodore—

JEFF

Pity you didn't enjoy alone time so much when you were / actually married.

DIANA
(to LIZZIE)

/ Lieutenant Elliot has gone completely insane, you know.

JEFF

Will you / let me TALK?

DIANA

/ I really have pity on the man.

JEFF

Your daughter is / right here, you know!

DIANA

/ I can't be angry at someone who thinks they're living in the year 2022!

JEFF

You're living in the year 2022!

OLIVE

It won't do any good.

DIANA

Yes, very good, Saunders, tell Ollie the truth now, and escort him to get some tea. His mother and I—

JEFF

Need some alone time. We know. Careful on the back, Lizzie, she can be a real animal when she feels like it.

LIZZIE

Wha—

OLIVE

Dad!

JEFF

We'll leave you two alone.

(OLIVE and JEFF exit.)

LIZZIE

It's time for her vitamins! I'm just—I'm just going to give her her vitamins!

Scene Two
(LIZZIE looks at DIANA.)

DIANA
(singing)
Whennnnnnn Brits are filling sea and sky,
When morale is low and seas are high--

LIZZIE
Oh, stop, my love.

DIANA
What is it, darling? How could you be in a sour mood after last night?

LIZZIE
They know!

DIANA
Know what, my love?

LIZZIE
Your lieutenants, your son, they *know* that we've, that we've, consummated our relationship.

DIANA
Well, yes, darling, I think it's assumed.

LIZZIE
Come on, please--

DIANA
Ollie isn't quite old enough to do the math, but I think when he grows up he'll realize—

LIZZIE
STOP!

DIANA

Whennnnnnn lieutenants are filling sea and sky—

LIZZIE

Very helpful.

DIANA

Sing with me, my love.

LIZZIE

"I cannot, my Oliver."

DIANA

Whyever not, my Elizabeth?

LIZZIE

They're talking behind our backs.

DIANA

Oh, don't give up the ship!
Oh, don't give up the ship!

LIZZIE

They're plotting in the kitchen. They don't trust me, they
think—

DIANA

When morale is low and seas are HIIIIIIIGHHHHH,
DON'T GIVE UP TH--

LIZZIE

SHUT UP, OLIVER!

DIANA

Well.

LIZZIE

My love, my only, Commodore of my heart, your lieutenants
are scheming to rid you of your command.

DIANA

To--

LIZZIE

They destroyed your room! And now *he's* here again, and—

DIANA

Darling.

LIZZIE

Whether they know or not—and it does seem like your
husband /

DIANA

/ Ex-husband—

LIZZIE

/ knows, they're sick of your command and they're—did you
just say "ex-husband"?

DIANA

I said nothing of the sort.

LIZZIE

You did. You said that Jeff is your ex-husband.

DIANA

I have no idea what you refer to, my love.

LIZZIE

You DO! You were here! You just said--

DIANA

Please, calm down, my Elizabeth. It is I, your Commodore, your Oliver Hazard Perry, in full uniform, in complete command.

LIZZIE

Truly?

DIANA

Would you like to waltz to prove it?

LIZZIE

Perhaps.

DIANA

Well, then, shall we?

> *(DIANA bows low and offers her hand to LIZZIE. No music, this time—they dance in silence.)*

Scene Three
> *(Lights up on the kitchen.)*

OLIVE

I told you it wasn't going to work.

MARTHA

You never said that.

OLIVE

I told you, she needs stability.

MARTHA

You were throwing things with the best of them!

                                JEFF
Girls.

                              MARTHA
You put your foot through that ugly picture—

                               OLIVE
YOU came up with the tacky lipstick idea—

                                JEFF
GIRLS! ...You called me with a plan, Martha.

                              MARTHA
Right. The plan.

                               OLIVE
Well? Did you go to the library?

                              MARTHA
Hang on. I have to set up.

                                JEFF
                          (aside to OLIVE)
Do you know what she's doing?

                               OLIVE
                          (aside to JEFF)
I didn't know there were props.

                                JEFF
Looks like we're getting what we paid for with that fancy
degree.

                    *(MARTHA pulls a few posterboards from behind
                    the table. On one, she has written and depicted
                    "MEETING ELIZABETH CHAMWOG." On the
                    second, she has written and depicted "BATTLE*

OF LAKE ERIE." On the third, she has depicted
"BIRTH OF OHP JR." On the fourth,
"VENEZUELA.")

OLIVE

You really take the presentation thing seriously, don't you.

MARTHA

Ahem! Listen up.

JEFF

All ears.

MARTHA

We have gathered here today to reclaim our mother (slash, ex-wife) from the grips of her identity crisis. To this end, I have assembled some data that track her "life" as Oliver Hazard Perry. I've discovered not only the logical patterns behind her delusions but also a potential solution.

Item One. The first thing she did was meet Elizabeth Whatsit at the ball. She cast Lizzie as her wife, probably to make Dad madly jealous, I'll get there in a moment, and got more into it once Lizzie reciprocated by pretending to be ECM.

Item Two. The next big event was the Battle of Lake Erie, which she played out in order to get at the relationship between Elliot and Perry, a.k.a. me and her. From Google—

OLIVE
(sighs loudly)

MARTHA

—I've ascertained that this whole thing boils down to the turning of the ships on Lake Erie. This makes complete sense, because in her deluded mind Mom could easily think that me not turning our "ship" around during the squall is what caused her to almost drown. She was shocked and traumatized by her near-drowning, and she needed to let that out and get mad at me. Check. That's done.

Item Three. The casting of Dad as her four-year-old son. This relates, in a twisted way, to the jealousy thing. What do four-year-olds do? They love unconditionally. What does Mom want Dad to do? Love her unconditionally. So, that's clearly where that's coming from.

Item Four. Venezuela.

OLIVE

"One of these things is not like the other."

MARTHA

Hush. In 1819, Secretary of the Navy Smith Thompson gave Oliver Hazard Perry a commission to go to Venezuela on a secret mission. Google thinks that he conducted diplomatic talks with Simon Bolivar. But—maybe most importantly— Venezuela is where Commodore Oliver Hazard Perry died from yellow fever. Where the Perry identity has to die.

OLIVE

So... you're trying to kill Mom?

MARTHA

Not Mom. Perry!

OLIVE

I think they're inhabiting the same body at the moment?

MARTHA

Look—I think you were right, Olive. Yesterday, before we—the key is not to mess things up. The key is stability, in a way. The key is to buy into her world so much that we use her own rules against her.

OLIVE

You want to hire a Smith Thompson?

MARTHA

We don't have to.

(MARTHA looks at her father.)

JEFF

Me? The person Diana hates most in the world?

MARTHA

No! Don't you see? In her delusions, *I'm* the person she hates most in the world! In her delusions, though, everyone—the evil Elliot, the awesome Saunders, the honorable Perry—they're all bound by the command of the United States Navy. Denying a commission would be denying Perry—

OLIVE

Which means denying that world. But it also means—

MARTHA

Will you stop it with the death stuff? It's not medically possible for her to die just because the voice in her head goes away!

OLIVE

Are you sure?

MARTHA

You're just scared.

OLIVE

Of course I'm scared!

JEFF

You want me to—

MARTHA

Pretend to be Smith Thompson, give Mom her commission
to go to Venezuela, and be there when she wakes up so that
you can sweep her into your arms, which is really what she's
wanted all along! It's obvious when you think about it.

JEFF

And you've obviously thought about it.

OLIVE

I guess you've done your research.

MARTHA
(to JEFF)

It was only going to work if you came back. But *you came
back*. You didn't leave us again.

JEFF
(to himself)

"Again."

MARTHA

Well?

OLIVE

What about Clarice?

MARTHA

There's that. But--

JEFF

...Don't worry about Clarice.

OLIVE

What?

JEFF

I'm here for you. For my daughters.

MARTHA

For... Mom.

JEFF

For Mom.

(MARTHA hugs JEFF.)

MARTHA

I knew it.

OLIVE

So—Dad—you're in?

JEFF

Smith Thompson at your service.

MARTHA

It could be worth it—if Mom really--

JEFF

You're crazier than she is, sweetheart. Diana isn't doing this because she loves me.

MARTHA

Isn't she?

OLIVE

I guess it kind of makes sense.

MARTHA

It really makes sense.

JEFF

You think she's doing this because she loves me?

MARTHA

She's too proud to ask directly. Maybe this is the only thing she could come up with.

JEFF

Well.

MARTHA

I think… I think she has always loved you.

> *(Lights fade on the kitchen. A spot comes up on DIANA and LIZZIE, still dancing silently, holding each other close.)*

Scene Four

> *(Martial music begins, first quietly, then loudly. DIANA kisses LIZZIE's hand and backs away from her to take her position aboard the "ship"/bed.)*

DIANA

My love, the high seas call Commodore Perry once more. The Barbary pirates call! They threaten our very existence, and they must be completely eradicated.

LIZZIE

But "why must you leave, my brave Commodore?"

DIANA

Fear not, my sweet one. I shall return. Off to the U.S.S. Java!
Off to the Mediterranean! Off, at last, to a straightforward
war that I—of course—shall win!

LIZZIE

"And you shall carry my handkerchief!"

> *(Triumphant music. LIZZIE tosses a pillowcase
> up to DIANA, and DIANA catches it
> dramatically and ties it around her neck like a
> cravat. DIANA swashbuckles showily.)*

DIANA

For you, my love, I shall be triumphant! Take that, pirate
one! Take that, pirate two! Look how easily I dispatch them,
my love! And pirate three, here we go!

> *(DIANA is in the middle of stabbing a third
> pirate who had been sneaking up on her from
> behind when JEFF, OLIVE, and MARTHA enter.
> JEFF has dressed himself in something that is
> meant to be a naval uniform from 1819. There
> may be a wig and tri-cornered hat involved.
> MARTHA and OLIVE also sport "naval
> uniforms," and MARTHA carries a device that
> loudly plays a song that drowns out DIANA's
> pirate theme music. For a few seconds, the two
> songs screech against each other, grating on
> everyone's ears—then, MARTHA's music wins
> out. Until noted, DIANA continues to fight
> imaginary pirates.)*

MARTHA

Announcing...

OLIVE

Now announcing...

DIANA

Ha! Pirate three dispatched!

MARTHA

The great (and stunningly handsome)...

OLIVE

Secretary of the United States Navy...

MARTHA

Smith Thompson!

LIZZIE
(to OLIVE and MARTHA)

What are you *doing*?

DIANA
(to an imaginary pirate)

Die, heathen!

MARTHA

Oh—Ms. Perry—your script. Do follow along.

> *(MARTHA hands LIZZIE a sheet of paper with her "lines" on it.)*

JEFF

I demand your salute, Commodore.

LIZZIE

My *script*? What are you doing, Martha?

DIANA

Die, heathen, die!

MARTHA
(to LIZZIE)
Buying in. (loudly) My name is Lieutenant Elliot of the
United States Navy, my lady.

JEFF
Once again, I demand your salute!

DIANA
(breaks away from her pirates)
You dunces, Smith Thompson isn't here. This is a PIRATE
SHIP.

JEFF
I beg to differ, Commodore. You will recognize your
superior officer.

DIANA
There are PIRATES everywhere. I cannot stop fighting!

OLIVE
Get Lizzie to read her line.

MARTHA
Stay in character. *(whispers to LIZZIE)* Ms. Perry, read your
line!

LIZZIE
(doubtfully)
"Oh, my husband, it is Secretary of the Navy Smith
Thompson." Martha--

MARTHA
Please address me as Lieutenant Elliot!

DIANA

Take that, heathen! Take that! A little help, Lieutenants?

JEFF

There are no pirates here, Commodore! You will recognize
your superior officer!

DIANA

I don't have a superior officer!

(DIANA points her sword at JEFF.)

That man is the last pirate standing.

MARTHA and OLIVE
(gasp very loudly)

LIZZIE

No need to resort to violence, my love--

MARTHA

You would break the chain of command?

OLIVE

You would deny the United States Navy?

LIZZIE

I'm sure there's a way we can—

JEFF

I am astonished at this breach of conduct.

DIANA

That man is clearly a pirate! Look at that hat! Saunders, I'm
surprised at you for having been taken in!

OLIVE

I'm surprised at you, Commodore! Put the sword down!

MARTHA

You are overstepping the regulations of the U. S. Navy!

LIZZIE

Gentlemen--

OLIVE

Article 14B, insubordination toward a superior officer!

MARTHA

Article 14B point 6, threat of violence toward a superior officer!

JEFF

Article 18 A point 5, not possessing the correct regulation sword!

OLIVE

All punishable by severe court-martial by a jury of your peers!

JEFF

There are three officers present, one a clear superior!

MARTHA

We have quorum for court-martial!

OLIVE

Must we resort to court-martial?

JEFF

Your salute or your resignation.

MARTHA

Do lend us your voice, Ms. Elizabeth Champlin Mason
Perry.

LIZZIE
(stage whisper)

Martha—

MARTHA

What would Elizabeth Champlin Mason Perry do?

LIZZIE

"Elliot"—"the surgeon doth not approve of this attempt"—

MARTHA
(referring to LIZZIE's script)
WHAT would Elizabeth Champlin Mason Perry do?

LIZZIE
(taking on the role, reading the line)
"O, gentlemen! Do not besmirch my husband's honor! He
must remain a commodore!"

MARTHA

Thank you.

> *(All wait for DIANA to reply. She is almost at a
> loss.)*

DIANA

Smith Thompson doesn't travel to the Mediterranean.

JEFF

Your salute or your resignation.

OLIVE

You dare not resign, Commodore.

DIANA

Venezuela doesn't happen until 1819.

MARTHA

Your salute or your resignation.

DIANA

You can't do this!

JEFF

On the contrary, my dear misguided Commodore, I am the Secretary of the Navy. I can do whatever I want. Your commission.

> *(JEFF proffers a piece of paper that has been tea-stained and is meant to look old. OLIVE ceremoniously offers it to MARTHA, who ceremoniously offers it to DIANA, then lays it at her feet.)*

If you recognize the authority of the United States Navy, my Commodore, you will recognize me. Your world depends on it. ...Your wife wouldn't love you if you weren't a Commodore, now would she?

LIZZIE

I will love Oliver to the end of the world and back.

MARTHA

Exactly. *Oliver.*

JEFF

Salute, Commodore.

MARTHA

Salute.

OLIVE

Salute.

(DIANA does, begrudgingly, salute.)

JEFF

Good Commodore. What a good little Commodore. "Come to Papa."

MARTHA

Read your commission, Commodore. And follow it to the letter.

(JEFF, MARTHA, and OLIVE exit. LIZZIE follows and grabs OLIVE.)

LIZZIE

What are you doing?

OLIVE

Trying something.

LIZZIE

Changing the rules on her?

OLIVE

Buying into her world!

LIZZIE

This isn't medically sound! This isn't—

OLIVE

You're the one who said to buy in!

LIZZIE

This isn't what I meant by—

116

OLIVE

We don't need to explain ourselves to you.

LIZZIE

You're starting to sound like Martha.

OLIVE

And you're starting to sound like Elizabeth Champlin Mason.
Which is weirder?

LIZZIE

Come on, Olive.

OLIVE

Come on, what?

LIZZIE

You're just falling in line behind Martha, just like—

OLIVE

I want my mother back. Don't you?

LIZZIE

...Of course.

OLIVE

Then get in there and send her to Venezuela.

LIZZIE

Venezuela.

OLIVE

It's all in the letter. ...And Lizzie?

LIZZIE

Yes?

OLIVE

For everyone's sake, including your own—you're a great
actor, but stop playing the part so well.

LIZZIE

…Yes, sir.

(OLIVE exits.)

Scene Five

*(In the bedroom, DIANA remains frozen in her
"salute." LIZZIE enters the bedroom.)*

DIANA

I am sorry, my love.

LIZZIE

Why are you sorry?

DIANA

I am sorry you had to see that.

LIZZIE

It's all part of your dutiful service to the United States Navy,
my love. I understand.

DIANA

Not to the Navy.

LIZZIE

Whatever do you mean, my darling?

DIANA

You know what I must mean, my love. I must take my leave
of you.

LIZZIE

...You're going to sea again? *(a joke)* I'm going to start running out of handkerchiefs.

DIANA

It is time for the battle that ends the war.

LIZZIE

But—already? The Barbary pirates just—you're supposed to have another three hundred pages.

DIANA

You have been a great comfort to me.

LIZZIE

"Have been."

DIANA

According to my lieutenants, I have been commissioned—

LIZZIE

To leave me.

DIANA

—to sail secretly to Venezuela to meet with the governor on a top-secret mission crucial to the economic well-being of the United States of America.

LIZZIE

Died. Venezuela, 1819.

DIANA

It's far, I know. It's almost to the end of the world.

LIZZIE

Born. Rhode Island, 1785. Died. Venezuela, 1819. Already?

DIANA

You're not making sense, my love.

LIZZIE

You're not considering taking this commission, are you?

DIANA

What?

LIZZIE

You've created a world for us! Why do you want to end it?

DIANA

Whatever do you mean?

LIZZIE

Oliver Hazard Perry dies in Venezuela!

DIANA

Now, that's a bit drastic of a worry, don't you think?

LIZZIE

It says. On Google. You know that.

DIANA
(ignoring modern language)
This, Lizzie, is the letter I have received from Secretary of the Navy Smith Thompson--

LIZZIE

I KNOW!

DIANA

Well, darling, you're a bit emphatic tonight.

LIZZIE

I know who Smith Thompson is, and I know you're going to
do what he says.

DIANA

I'm not leaving because of Smith Thompson.

LIZZIE

He is your "superior officer."

DIANA

My darling--

LIZZIE

Is he not?

DIANA

No! ...If Smith Thompson only had asked me to go, I would
have laughed in his face. But my lieutenants were not
laughing. They need me to go--

LIZZIE

So you're giving up?

DIANA

My lieutenants love me, Lizzie. They offer faithful service. I
must serve them in return.

LIZZIE

You never said this was temporary.

DIANA

Oh, sweetheart.

LIZZIE

You said our souls would be—

DIANA

My country calls me.

LIZZIE

You SAID!

DIANA

My lieutenants...

LIZZIE

You said…

DIANA

There will be other worlds.

> *(DIANA tries to embrace LIZZIE. LIZZIE moves away.)*

You're angry.

LIZZIE

Of course I'm angry.

DIANA

Why, truly?

LIZZIE

Think about it.

DIANA

I will find you when I return from South America.

LIZZIE

No, you won't!

DIANA

I will!

LIZZIE
You know you won't. …You can't have us both. You said—
you can't have us both.

DIANA
I can try.

LIZZIE
And *this* is how you try?

DIANA
What would you have me do?

LIZZIE
Let's go together.

DIANA
What?

LIZZIE
Let's go to Venezuela! Together! Let's go to the airport and
fly standby and figure out the twenty-first century on the
plane!

DIANA
What?

LIZZIE
We'll get on this newfangled invention thing that has wings
and soars through the air, far away--

DIANA
You suggest something that sounds insane, my darling.

LIZZIE
Really? *Air travel* is what sounds insane?

DIANA

Do you wish me to break my promise to my lieutenants?

LIZZIE

I have given you everything—

DIANA

Do you wish me to break my promise to my lieutenants?

LIZZIE

I don't know.

DIANA

My honor / must remain intact.

LIZZIE

/ And what about my honor? Do you realize what I've / given you?

DIANA

Do you realize what I owe my family?

LIZZIE

I hate your family.

DIANA

I love my family. …My naval family.

LIZZIE

They are nothing but cruel to you! They are hurtful and selfish and cruel! And you leave me because of a letter?

DIANA

When I am truly summoned, I must go. ...I love you,
Elizabeth. I will love you even if Mister Smith Thompson
tells me I cannot. I will love you in Rhode Island, in
Venezuela, and in heaven. I will love you beyond all love,
for all time. Believe me.

LIZZIE

But when he calls, you jump.

DIANA

It's not *him.*

LIZZIE

Bullshit.

DIANA

I swear to you, it's not—

LIZZIE

I'm saying *this* is bullshit. You get me to—you get me to fall
in love with you, with this dashing man in uniform, but then
with you, with, with, and then you just throw me out? Are
you insane? Are you really insane? Do you have any idea
what this is doing to me?

DIANA

Lizzie—

LIZZIE

Stop. Stop it. Stop saying my name, stop—

DIANA

Please calm down.

LIZZIE

Calm down? *Calm down*? Calming down doesn't get anyone anything in this house, does it? No, you gotta put on a tricornered hat instead and turn up the crazy. That's how you get what you want. It's how you got what *you* wanted, which now I'm guessing was just—was just—

DIANA

I wanted *you*.

LIZZIE

Yeah, I'm getting sick of the past tense. You know what? I think I'll pick a new identity, too. That fixes everything, right? Makes everything a-okay? You're gonna leave, I'll pick, um… Elvis, maybe. Wanna make love to Elvis? That swoopy hair, he looked kinda like a girl—you seem to have a thing for girls—

DIANA

I just—

LIZZIE

I'm not DONE! Do you think I'm done? Do I look like I'm done? You listen to Nurse Lizzie's plan. Okay? You sit back and listen and I'll take care of everything, just like always, just like all the other residential nurses from the twenty-first century. You're gonna go back to being Diana. Fine. Because apparently you've made that decision. And it's gonna be oh so bittersweet and lovely for your dedicated asshole daughters. And then, oh, wait for it, then, next weekend I'm gonna go swimming in Narragansett Bay and knock my head on a rock and come up singing Burning Love. And I'll need a nurse! I'll need a dedicated nurse who caters to my every whim. And I do mean *every whim*, know what I'm saying? And I'll have to look to my friends and neighbors, of course, because I don't have any money, you remember that part? Because, of course, this was my job? Residential nursing

LIZZIE (cont)
care was gonna be my job? And now? After this? Your
daughter is gonna take me and run my name through seven
types of mud and ten types of shit, you think I'm gonna have
a job anymore? You think I can do the thing I've been
studying for and paying for, that I have all these ridiculous
loans for? And you don't *want* me?

DIANA
I do want you. After—please. If you can just—

LIZZIE
There is no after. Are you listening? After this, *there is no
after*.

*(DIANA lunges at LIZZIE and kisses her,
roughly.)*

DIANA
(repeats her question for the last time)
Do you want me to break my promise *to my lieutenants*?

LIZZIE
If that's the question you're gonna ask… if you have to
ask… then no.

DIANA
I would.

LIZZIE
Oh, my "dashing and honorable Commodore." You would
not.

(LIZZIE starts to exit. DIANA holds out a hand.)

DIANA
One last dance, my love? Come waltz with me.

LIZZIE

…Elvis doesn't waltz.

(LIZZIE exits.)

(DIANA brings her hand down. She processes to the bed and lies down.)

DIANA

Seventeen horses, four carriages, three cities all in black. The mayor of Newport, the mayor of Kansas City, the mayor of Cincinnati. His wife Elizabeth Champlin Mason Perry. His four children, Christopher Grant, Oliver, Christopher Raymond, Elizabeth. His right-hand lieutenants. Even his enemies mourned.

Scene Six

(Lights up on MARTHA, OLIVE, and JEFF in the kitchen.)

MARTHA

She saluted.

JEFF

She did.

MARTHA

Maybe I was right.

JEFF

Maybe you were right.

OLIVE

If she's adhering to the text…

DIANA
(from her room, loudly)
SEVENTEEN HORSES.

*(MARTHA and JEFF run toward DIANA's room.
OLIVE is in the hall.)*

OLIVE

Come on!

DIANA

FOUR CARRIAGES.

MARTHA

Is she--

OLIVE

It's the funeral procession.

JEFF

Perry's funeral procession.

OLIVE

Page four hundred and seventy-three.

DIANA

THREE CITIES ALL IN BLACK!

Scene Seven
*(All enter DIANA's room. DIANA is lying on the
bed.)*

MARTHA

Mom!

                         JEFF

Diana?

                         OLIVE

Mom!

                         DIANA
                (sits up straight and shouts)
The mayor of Newport the mayor of Kansas City the mayor
of Cincinnati!

                *(She falls back on the bed, limp. She does not
                move or wake.)*

                        MARTHA

What's happening?

                         OLIVE

Mom! Why isn't she waking up?

                        MARTHA

Where's Lizzie? Lizzie!

                         OLIVE

Lizzie!

                         JEFF

Does she need CPR?

                        MARTHA

How would I know?

                         OLIVE

Oh Jesus Christ. What is happening? What is HAPPENING?

                         JEFF

I can give her CPR.

130

OLIVE
Do you KNOW CPR? LIZZIE!

MARTHA
LIZZIE!

(LIZZIE enters.)

Where have you been?

LIZZIE
Move back.

MARTHA
She could be dying, here—

LIZZIE
Move back!

*(LIZZIE performs CPR on DIANA. DIANA
wakes and turns the CPR into a kiss, holding
LIZZIE's head there.)*

MARTHA
Whoa! Mom!

OLIVE
Is she / kissing Lizzie?

MARTHA
/ She's still crazy! Get away from her!

DIANA
(staring deeply into LIZZIE's eyes)
His wife Elizabeth Champlin Mason Perry.

LIZZIE

Diana?

MARTHA

Get away from her.

LIZZIE

I'm trying!

> *(LIZZIE pulls away and purposefully wipes her mouth and pretends disgust at the kiss.)*

DIANA
> *(turns to Jeff)*

His four children, Christopher Grant, Oliver, Christopher Raymond, Elizabeth.

JEFF

She's still—she's still—

LIZZIE

Wait.

DIANA
> *(turns to MARTHA and OLIVE, takes their hands)*

His right-hand lieutenants. Even his enemies mourned.

MARTHA

Mom?

OLIVE

Mom?

DIANA

August 23, 1819. Did you know that? That's when he died?

OLIVE

He?

DIANA

Commodore Oliver Hazard Perry, silly. Who else would I be talking about?

OLIVE

Thank God.

MARTHA

Thank God. Oh, thank God!

JEFF

Diana?

MARTHA

It's 2022.

DIANA

I know.

OLIVE

Your name is Diana.

DIANA

I know.

MARTHA

You have some of your nurse's lipstick on your mouth.

DIANA

I know.

LIZZIE

Clearly she was still in the delusion—but now she seems—

MARTHA

Yes. Sorry about the--mess. She clearly didn't—you didn't—

LIZZIE

That's never happened before. The stress of waking up—

OLIVE

Right.

LIZZIE

She seems stable. I should go.

DIANA

Stay.

LIZZIE

It'll be easier for her to transition out of the delusion if I'm
not around. She sees me as—well, clearly, something I'm
not. It'll be easier if… You'll want to have a family reunion,
and I'll just be—call me if
she—she'll be fine.

DIANA

Lizzie. Stay.

MARTHA

Mom, let her / go.

OLIVE

Martha, let her finish.

DIANA

I meant to kiss you, Lizzie. You know that.

LIZZIE

I don't know anything, Diana. The kissing is clearly
inappropriate.

DIANA

I'm sorry if I offended you.

LIZZIE

You should be. …I mean—Martha—I'll take my last check by mail, if that's all right?

OLIVE

Lizzie, / wait.

MARTHA

/ Of course. Our apologies. Really.

OLIVE

Martha—

JEFF

Thank you for your service to our family.

LIZZIE

Of course.

DIANA

Lizzie—

LIZZIE

Don't focus on your delusions, Diana. It's healthiest for you now to forget what you thought was true and just go back to your real life. Talk to your daughters, Diana. Tell them how much they mean to you. Promise me that you'll do that. Focus on 2022. Focus on them. …Not on me.

DIANA

I promise.

(LIZZIE exits.)

MARTHA

You promise? You promise what?

OLIVE

Mom, are you sure you're—you?

DIANA

I'm me.

OLIVE

I missed you.

(DIANA holds out her arms and OLIVE and
MARTHA rush to hug her.)

MARTHA

...How much do you remember?

DIANA

I remember the bay.

OLIVE

You fell overboard.

MARTHA

And?

DIANA

I don't know. Keep hugging.

MARTHA

But—

DIANA

What?

JEFF

What about Lizzie? That's what your daughters want to know, Diana. What about Lizzie?

DIANA

I kissed her. I meant to do it.

OLIVE

You meant to do it. Okay.

MARTHA

Dear God.

DIANA

She is a beautiful woman.

OLIVE

She does have nice hair.

MARTHA

You're wrong! You didn't—

DIANA

I did. I kissed Lizzie. As myself.

MARTHA

You didn't!

OLIVE

Look, Martha, maybe you should stop telling people what they did and didn't do!

DIANA

I love her.

(JEFF begins to laugh.)

DIANA (cont)

What is so funny?

JEFF

Of course that's it. Of course, Diana. You *would* find a way
to humiliate me even more than you already have.

DIANA

This has nothing to do with you.

JEFF

That girl—you told her she was pretty? And she just—

DIANA

Lizzie didn't do anything. …She's my nurse, nothing more.
She did her job. She doesn't love me.

OLIVE

But you… love her.

DIANA

Yes. …I do.

> *(JEFF exits suddenly, slamming the door behind
> him.)*

MARTHA

Dad!

OLIVE

Martha, calm down.

MARTHA

Mom! Look what you did! Dad—

DIANA

Let him go.

MARTHA

Let him GO? But you—

DIANA

I love Lizzie.

MARTHA

Will you stop fixating on that? It's not like your delusions
mattered!

OLIVE

Right. Because you get to decide what matters to everyone
else.

MARTHA

They didn't matter, right, Mom?

DIANA

Martha—

MARTHA

If they didn't matter, and everything can come back to—if
you can come back to us, then we can forgive you, right,
Olive? Mom, we can forgive you.

DIANA

Forgive me for what?

MARTHA

For what? For WHAT? For LEAVING, Mom. For not taking
my hand. For calling me a coward. For pushing me over. For
ordering Olive around. For insulting our father. For
KISSING Lizzie. For taking the sacrament, the sacrament
you KNOW is holy and true and IMPORTANT TO ME, and
mocking it! For mocking God! For mocking me!

DIANA

I've been cruel to you. ...I'm sorry.

OLIVE

Thank you.

MARTHA

Thank y—

DIANA

But I can't apologize for Lizzie.

MARTHA

Oh, she can say she's sorry another time. She did get a little too wrapped up in the acting, and clearly that deluded you, made you fall into this weird fantasy—but I don't think she *meant* to—

DIANA

She didn't do anything wrong. ...I won't apologize for loving her.

OLIVE

You tell her, Mom.

MARTHA
(to OLIVE)

Why are *you* all self-righteous?

DIANA

My name is Diana. I am the mother of two beautiful and intelligent and compassionate daughters. I was once married to their father, but I am not anymore. I live in Narragansett, Rhode Island, I know a lot about Commodore Oliver Hazard Perry, and I am in love with a woman. I have kissed her, I have—I have dreamed of making love to her, and I love her.

MARTHA

Jesus Christ our Lord.

DIANA

And I left her. / For you, Martha.

MARTHA

/ Jesus Christ our Lord, / how have I sinned?

DIANA

/ I looked my love in the eye, and I left her company to come be your mother / again.

MARTHA

/ I beg forgiveness / for my mother, who has lost her way. I beg forgiveness for my mother, who has lost her way. I beg forgiveness for my mother--

DIANA

/ I left my own world behind to live in yours. So I beg you to stop calling on your God and make your peace with me.

MARTHA

I don't—I can't--

DIANA

Make your peace with me.

(DIANA holds out her arms.)

Please.

MARTHA

But you love DAD!

OLIVE

No. She doesn't.

MARTHA

This whole time, you were making Dad jealous. You just
wanted him to love you unconditionally. You need to go after
him, you need to—you need to catch him at the airport, you
need to--

DIANA

Sweetheart... I don't love your father.

MARTHA

Then why wake up?

OLIVE

Jesus Christ, are you that / single-minded?

MARTHA

/ If you were having such a great time in Perry-land, then
why did you wake up? Why didn't you just STAY in your
own selfish little world?

DIANA

Because—listen to me. Because no matter who I choose,
Martha, I will always choose you. And Olive.

MARTHA

Even if--

DIANA

Even if you damn my soul. You will always be the only ones
I cannot live without.

MARTHA

...I can't live without you, either.

DIANA

You don't have to.

(A moment. Then MARTHA gathers herself away and becomes practical.)

MARTHA

…You need rest.

OLIVE

We all need some rest.

MARTHA

And tea. …I'll make you some tea.

(MARTHA exits.)

OLIVE
(to DIANA)
So you were in there? The whole time?

DIANA
(tenderly)
Ollie… you should go after your sister.

(OLIVE goes to her mother and hugs her for a long moment. Then OLIVE exits after MARTHA.)

Scene Eight

(DIANA rests for a moment, then gets up and picks up the cardboard box. She takes the picture off of the wall and places it in the box. She moves to the figure of a sailor, picks it up. She places the sailor figurine in the box. She picks up the Perry book. She lets the book fall into the box.)

DIANA

It doesn't feel like much, does it, Lizzie?

(DIANA turns on the song that she and LIZZIE waltzed to.)

Mrs. Champlin Mason Perry, may I have this dance?

(She bows and pretends to take LIZZIE's hand. MARTHA enters, carrying a cup of tea, but stops abruptly when she sees her mother.)

You look so beautiful with that bashful blush on your cheek.

(DIANA dances, holding up her arms to frame another person's shoulders. MARTHA watches her dance.)

MARTHA
So he's still here. The Commodore.

DIANA
Oh, Martha. I was always here.

(MARTHA puts the cup of tea down on the side table. She goes to the boombox and shuts off DIANA's waltz music. She exits.)

(DIANA resumes her dance. As lights fade, she sings softly:)
DIANA
Don't give up the ship, *Diana*,
Don't give up the ship.
When morale is low and seas are hiiiigh--
Don't give up... the...

(Fade to black.)
(End of play.)